I0438113

RECALCULATIONS ON PEACE AND EMERGING NATIONS

By

Kelly NGYAH, PhD

Research & Working Papers Initiative towards
Global Peace and Development @ MAHSRA
Publications 2015

Content

Introduction

Several recent world reports have commented on the upcoming of a new world order that though in line with the major global governance perspectives may greatly influence the general sociopolitical and economy structure of the globe. Building on very strong regional policies for the accommodation of solidified economic growth amongst member countries and the need to strengthen peaceful operations, national solidarity, and build mutually beneficial bilateral trade partnerships within other developing countries, a set of five emerging nations have opted for the institution of a global order financial development structure that would set a pace for achieving their goals.

As countries which have instituted firm internal and foreign policies to promote global peace processes especially at the regional levels of their continents, there have been several purports to evaluate the extent to which these emerging nations can modify the cause of peace globally. This study therefore attempts in understanding the classical distinction of nations within the developed and developing stances in order to distinguish the 'emerging nation' concept. It as well indicates the values within the emerging nation's conception that contribute to in-country and regional or global peace. From an overview on the examples of emerging nations their historical construe towards achieving in-country peaceful governance and stability and their prospective polices and already contributed practices within several regional conflicts are analyzed. It thus focuses a forecast on the BRICS future impact in world peace.

The Statistical Distinction of an Emerging Nation from an Economy Variance Perspective

From its definitional perspective, an emerging nation is a country that is on its way towards becoming an industrialized nation or a developing country and that has achieved some industrial capacity like Brazil and India.[1] Meanwhile an industrialized country or a developed country or "more developed country" (MDC), is considered as a sovereign State that has a highly developed economy and advanced technological infrastructure relative to other less developed nations, a developing country also called a less-developed country (LDC),[2] is

---

[1] Sourced:
http://www.hanisauland.de/en/en_lexicon/en_e/emerging-nation.html

[2] Sourced: Financial Dictionary http://financial-dictionary.thefreedictionary.com/lesauthor=Farlex Financial Dictionary

a nation with a low living standard, underdeveloped industrial base, and low Human Development Index – HDI (Created by Pakistani economist Mahbub ul Haq, followed by economist Amartya Sen in 1990,[3] and published by the United Nations Development Programme[4]: the Human Development Index (HDI) is a composite statistic of life expectancy, education, and income indices to rank countries into four tiers of human development) relative to other countries.[5] Also, developed countries are composite of an economy system in which the service sector provides more wealth than the Industrial sector and is a characteristic of post-industrialized economies but the

---

[3] 'The Human Development concept'. Available online at: http://hdr.undp.org/en/humandev/ Retrieved 7 April 2012.

[4] See www.undp.org/content/undp/en/home.html

[5] See Sullivan, Arthur; Steven M. Sheffrin (2003).

developing or the under developed countries
are mostly fundamental of agrarian economies
which are still at a pre-industrial level and
still   undergoing   the   process   of
industrialization.

There are no universal, agreed-upon
criteria for what makes a country developing
versus developed and which countries fit these
two categories but the common generally used
reference points such as the size of a nation's
GDP compared to other nations. According to
the International Monetary Fund, advanced
economies comprise 65.8% of global nominal
GDP and 52.1% of global GDP (PPP) in 2010.[6]
In 2011, the ten largest advanced economies
by either nominal GDP or GDP (PPP) are the

---

[6] See IMF GDP data (September 2011), Available online at:
http://www.imf.org/external/pubs/ft/weo/2011/02/weodata/
weorept.aspx?pr.x=30&pr.y=7&sy=1980&ey=2016&scsm=1&ss
d=1&sort=country&ds=.&br=1&c=001%2C110&s=NGDPD%2CP
PPGDP%2CPPPSH&grp=1&a=1

United States, Germany, France, the United Kingdom, Japan, Italy, Canada, Spain and South Korea.[7] However, though the criteria for evaluating the degree of economic development is the gross domestic product (GDP), others such as the per capita income, level of industrialization, amount of widespread infrastructure and general standard of living[8] are also criteria employed in the distinction process. As such, classification of a country as being developed is still possible even when the GDP is presented otherwise. This comes from the fact that the IMF uses a flexible classification system that considers different indexes such as per capita income level, export diversification, and the degree of integration

---

[7] See IMF (2012).

[8] See http://www.investopedia.com/terms/d/developed-economy.asp#axzz1legO8olO

into the global financial system. In the calculative processes some lapses or poor performances against one sector towards the other may produce different values in the final calculations for example: in the case of export diversification considerations, oil exporters that have high per capita GDP would not make the advanced classification because around 70% of their exports are only oil.[9]

The World Bank's own classification puts country economies according to their GNI per capita income ranges into income groups each year on July 1 accordingly: In 2011 countries with US$12,476 GNI and above were considered as high income countries; those with GNI per capita between US$4,036 and US$12,476 considered upper middle income countries; those with GNI per capita between

---

[9] See IMF (2009).

US$1,026 and US$4,036 considered lower middle income countries; and those with US$1,026 and below considered low income countries. Though the implications of such a calculation was to the effect that all low-income and middle-income countries were to be considered as developing countries, ' 'the use of the term is convenient; it is not intended to imply that all economies in the group are experiencing similar development or that other economies have reached a preferred or final stage of development. Classification by income does not necessarily reflect development status.'[10]

The varying distinctions presented above are on the extreme angles of the scale and non-considerate of other categories of

---

[10] See 'How we Classify Countries'. Available online at:
http://data.worldbank.org/about/country-classifications. World
Bank. Retrieved on 28th of May 2013

economies that may fall in between the extreme classification lines. From other perspectives, the concept of a developing nation is also used in numerous theoretical systems within diverse orientations based on stereotypical conceptions on historical nation-states' evolution and literary divides across other national economy ideologies. For example: theories of decolonization, liberation theology, Marxism, anti-imperialism, and political economy. However, the United Nations Statistics Division acknowledges that there is no established convention for the designation of 'developed' and 'developing' countries or areas in the United Nations system[11]and also that 'the designations

---

[11] See 'Composition of macro geographical (continental) regions, geographical sub-regions, and selected economic and other groupings (footnote C)'. United Nations Statistics Division. revised 17 October 2008. Available online at:
http://unstats.un.org/unsd/methods/m49/m49regin.htm#ftnc
Retrieved on the 28th of May 2013.

"developed" and "developing" are intended for statistical convenience and do not necessarily express a judgment about the stage reached by a particular country or area in the development process'[12]. The countries which according to the distinctions are not found amongst the extreme angles need to be situated with the global development mapping index chart as well. This is in particular to countries with more advanced economies than other developing nations but that have not yet demonstrated signs of a developed country. In some instances they are often categorized as newly industrialized nations[13] meanwhile the most recent appellation regards them as

---

[12] See 'United Nations Statistics Division- Standard Country and Area Codes Classifications (M49)'. Available online at: http://unstats.un.org/unsd/methods/m49/m49.htm. retrieved on the 28th of May 2013

[13] See Paweł Bożyk (2006); Mauro F. Guillén (2003); Waugh, David (3rd edition 2000); Mankiw, N. Gregory (4th Edition 2007)

emerging nations. The typical examples of the emerging nations include the 'BRICS' countries, Brazil, Russia, India, China and South Africa which are difficult to categorize because of their rapid economic development in recent years. However, they are still not developed countries.

Values Contributing to Peace in Emerging Nations

The economic growth within emerging nations induces several advantages for citizenry wellbeing through systemic liberal governance and livelihood perspectives. When the citizens feel contented in one sector or the other or feel satisfied for one reason or the other, in the case of differences, they may intend only engage in non-emotional conflicts that are usually resolved only through peaceful measures. Some of these peace contributor values are highlighted according to the following instances.

The Middle Class Concerns

The middle classes within a nation are described from several views. Sociologically, the middle class also called bourgeoisie is a social stratum that is not clearly defined but is positioned between the lower and upper classes.

It consists of businessmen, professional people, etc., along with their families, and is marked by bourgeois values.[14] Considered as a class of people in the middle of the society, from another perspective and in Weberian socio-economic terms, middle class is the broad group of people in contemporary society who fall socio-economically between the working class and upper class with common measures varying significantly among their cultures. It also entails a class of people intermediate between those of higher and lower economic or social standing, generally characterized by average income and education, conventional values, and conservative attitudes.[15]

The middle classes which are mostly the majority in emerging nations are those who

---

[14] See http://www.thefreedictionary.com/middle+class

[15] Ibid.

contribute most in stabilizing the society through their activities and critical or pacifist comprehension of the nations governance mechanisms. As a result of the rapid growth in emerging countries, a new and more solicited view of the middle class has been reported. Announcing in February 2009 that over half the world's population now belongs to the middle class, *'The Economist'*[16] characterizes the middle class as having a reasonable amount of discretionary income, so that they do not live from hand to mouth as the poor do, and defined it as beginning at the point where people have roughly a third of their income left for discretionary spending after paying for basic food and shelter thus allowing people to buy consumer goods, improve their health care, and provide for their children's education. However,

---

[16] See https://en.wikipedia.org/wiki/The_Economist

even though the middle class people in the emerging world possess such a relative purchasing power sufficiency, they are still classified middle-class by the standards of the developing world but not the rich one, since their monetary incomes do not match developed country levels, but the percentage of it which is discretionary does. By this definition, the number of middle-class people in Asia exceeded that in the West sometime around 2007 or 2008.[17] These majority classes of persons in the society are therefore inclined to be satisfied within the nation else their collective actions may lead to serious political and economic destabilization of the society. Thus, the concept of peace within emerging nations is held by principles and values that integrate and fulfill the aspiration of the middle class, described accordingly:

---

[17] See Parker, John (2009-02-12)

1) *Democracy*. With respect to the democratic peace theories, the definition of democracy is tuned in different directions but its definitional approach will be limited to the present scope which concerns how its values are held amongst the middle classes within an emergent nation. From Doyle's perspectives he requires that (1) 'liberal régimes' have market or private property economics, (2) they have policies that are internally sovereign, (3) they have citizens with juridical rights, and (4) they have representative governments.[18] At the first (1) aspect, we can determine that democracy is a promoter of liberal marketing policies which of course are catalytic factors for encouraging private

---

[18] See Doyle, Michael W. (1983).

investments and individual returns benefits to the satisfaction of the investors. This therefore, on the other way round, means that economic well-being is linked with support for democracy. However, this does not imply that only the wealthy endorse democracy – on the contrary, support for democracy is solid in both rich and poor countries, and among both rich and poor respondents. However, it is especially strong among members of the global middle class. The results of this inter-connected and reciprocated relationship between democracy and middle class citizenry wellbeing can only as much as it stays on equal legality platforms, sustain stable peace and maintain the constant growth of the society. Banerjee and Duflo[19] note the links between the middle class and democracy—if democracy is then causally linked with growth, one can infer that the middle class causes growth. Since democracy acts as the most probable source of governance within emerging nations, therefore the situational peace and growth of such a nation can be looked upon as a political phenomenon in the hands of middle classes' choice. However, Barro (1996) finds only a weak (and slightly negative) impact of democracy on economic growth in a panel regression of 100 countries from 1960 to 1990, conditional on maintenance of the rule of law, free markets, small government consumption and high human capital.[20] There is

[19] See Banerjee, A. and E. Duflo (2007).

[20] See Barro, R. (1996).

however also other opinions with regards democracy and the middle class within countries other than the emerging nations. The Global Middle Class release writes that:

> In his widely read 2003 book, *The Future of Freedom*, Fareed Zakaria wrote about the world's growing number of 'illiberal democracies" – countries, often relatively poor countries, where elections take place, but individual rights, the rule of law, and other features of what he calls "constitutional liberalism' are absent. '[W]hen countries become democratic at low levels of development their democracy usually dies,' explains Zakaria.

Journalist Robert Kaplan has argued that since the end of the Cold War, elections have been held in the Balkans, Africa, Central Asia and elsewhere in nations that were not ready for democracy. According to Kaplan and others, such premature elections often lead to widespread violence or authoritarianism.[21]

The example mentioned above is to explain the fact that, it is not in every situation that democracy serves as an instrument for peace and growth. Comparably with the instances of the emerging nation, I have struggled to explain the fact that, because democracies provide liberal economic activities and at least minimum levels of satisfactory livelihood for the

---

[21] See The Global Middle Class (2009: 2).

majority of the populations which are indeed the middle classes, the popular will to kick against government agendas are usually weakened. For the case of poor and under developed countries wherein almost every citizen (lower, middle and/or upper) classes hold grievances against the government policies, marginal individual wage packages and a rather conservative economic system, there is bound to be intense conflicts and severe violent clashes. This is because whether one finds his/herself in the government or in the opposition, almost everyone feels unfulfilled or lacking in one aspect or the other. When personal satisfaction is not guaranteed within any society, the society is bound to host tensions between the providers, the distributors and the consumers.

In a countdown, the objective focus of all mentioned economic growth and personal satisfaction are merely the instances introduced to demonstrate on the issue that democratic values within an emerging nation, brings individual satisfaction, at least to a self-contentment level, and it is this self contentment value that promotes the maintainability of peace within the emerging nations.

2) *Religion*. When regarded as a system of believes through which people show, conceive and demonstrate allegiance to a deity or deities and divine involvement in the universe and human life, the people of the middle class society are largely less concerned or insensible to issues of religion which of course are basic moral catalyst for sustaining peace in a society. The Global Attitude Project's research on the middle class peoples' opinions to

believe in God, in moral values and the
value of good' gave the following results:[22]

> ...gaps exist in largely Hindu
> India (middle class – 60% very
> important; lower income – 72%).
> In Malaysia, which is majority
> Muslim but has significant
> Buddhist, Christian, and Hindu
> minorities, 60% of the middle class
> said religion is very important to
> them compared with 86% to those
> at the lower income level or class.

The statistics prove that in emerging
nations both the middle and the lower
income classes show equally weakened
tendencies towards the inclination on
religious principles but to a higher
extend, this tendency is mostly exhibited

---

[22] Ibid : 5

at the level of the middle class. The worry here is that, values of peace are mostly centered within the peripherals of moral descents but these same values are of limited importance amongst the middle class of people within the emerging nations who form the majority of the population. However, from the religious perspective, we may say that the societal stability and peaceful order that reigns amongst the middle classes in emerging nations is most probably based on the fact that they are united within believe systems. These systems are based on economic advantages as their adopted lifestyles and their most prominent existentiality focus through which they obtain satisfaction and have thus made it some sort of a religion for them. This idea ties with a part comprehensiveness of the notion of religion elaborated in the Encyclopedia of Philosophy's listed trait values that point at the definition of religion:[23]

- A world view or a general picture of the world as a whole and the place of the individual therein. This picture contains some specification of an over-all purpose or point of the world and an indication of how the individual fits into it;

- A more or less total organization of one's life based on the world view; and

- A social group bound together by the above.

---

[23] Source: "Agnosticism / Atheism: What is Religion? The Problem of Definition. The Difficulty with Defining Religion," About.com, at: http://atheism.about.com/

Thus, as well as democracy promotes liberal markets within emerging nations to the profit of the middle classes so is the believe in the individual wellbeing as a results of such liberal state of affairs that induces a new form of believe systems based on 'self-satisfaction interest' within the progressive economies.

An Institutionalized Peaceful Development Tract

This aspect is in relative concordances with the national policies and practices that are designed and directed towards promoting globalization and achievements in collaborative undertakings between intranational and international affairs. Considering China as an exemplary emerging nation that highly exhibits such an institutional strategy, the State Council of the People's Republic of China issued a white paper in 2005 defining the *China's peaceful development* strategy in theory and in practice with five chapters that are to the following effects:[24]

1) China is the largest developing country, and economic development according to globalization is China's main goal. China seeks a multipolar world rather than hegemony, and seeks relations with other countries based on Principles of Peaceful Open Cooperative and Harmonious Coexistence expressed thus:

   - Striving for a peaceful international environment to develop itself, and promoting world peace through its own development;

   - Achieving development by relying on itself, together with

---

[24] See People's Daily (2005-10-22).

reform and innovation, while
persisting in the policy of
opening-up;

- Conforming to the trend of
economic globalization, and
striving to achieve mutually
beneficial common development
with other countries;

- Sticking to peace, development
and cooperation, and, together
with all other countries,
devoting itself to building a
harmonious world marked by
sustained peace and common
prosperity

2) Seeking to promote world peace and
development with China's own growth is
as in: the reduction of poverty in the
world via its huge factories; reduce its

energy consumption; lessened the effects of the world recession; and concentrate on their own construction and whole-heartedly seek development, and strive constantly to make positive contributions to world peace and development with their own growth, and promote human civilization and progress;

3) Seeking to develop science by relying on its own strength, reform and innovation. It adheres to innovations in ideas and systems, opening up domestic market and pave a new path to industrialization that is cleaner, and makes more use of information technology and innovation by exploiting its human capital through education;

4) Seeking common benefits and development with other countries thus

remaining open to the outside world for trade. It will promote organizations like the World Trade Organization, and support regional integration through institutions like the China-ASEAN Free Trade Area. It will address trade and exchange rate conflicts on an equal footing with other countries. China will invest abroad and maintain its large labor force and exports for use abroad;

5) China will promote 'democracy in international relations'; with countries interacting on an equal footing through dialog and multilateralism and not coercion. China will promote the full participation of developing countries in international affairs, and also help them develop themselves. There should be trust and not a "cold war mentality", and arms

control and nuclear disarmament should be pursued. China will resolve its remaining border disputes peacefully.

In quest for peace within its territorial limits, China systematically and institutionally addressed most major conflict driving factors within its localities and amoungst its tribal people by instituting the system of regional ethnic autonomy, for example:

> In order to prevent ethnic fighting, China established a system of regional autonomy in order to protect the religions, culture, customs and living habits of ethnic minorities. This legally stipulated that principal officials of all levels of governments in the ethnic autonomous regions should be from minority groups. China's autonomous regions enjoy various preferential

policies and any discriminative words or conducts are strictly banned and subject to legal punishment. The system of regional ethnic autonomy not only ensures China's territorial integrity and national harmony; it also ensures that ethnic languages, cultural and religious heritage enjoy full preservation and further development.[25]

Also with China's recent plans to boost its economical development by promoting the urbanization and integration of its rural and urban construction, and also steadily push forward its political reforms, the country has strategically instituted appropriate mechanisms for strengthening its grassroots self-administration via cultural development concerns that encompasses four aspects as in:[26]

---

[25] See Qu Xing (2013)

- Constructing the socialist core values system with Chinese characteristics, which include prosperity, democracy, civility, and harmony, uphold freedom, equality, justice and the rule of law and advocate patriotism, dedication, integrity, and friendship, among other values;

- Improving civic morality in an all-around way by intensifying education in public morality, professional ethics, family virtues, and individual integrity;

- Enriching people's intellectual and cultural lives; and

- Enhancing the overall strength and international competitiveness of Chinese culture.

---

[26] Ibid.

These Chinese reforms upon cultural systems that are deepened so as to liberate cultural productivity within the country are therefore high promoter factors for dissolving ethnic divides and enhancing peaceful solidarity coexistence between its people.

With the example of another emerging nation such as Brazil, in contrast to the institutionalized peace development tract as that of China, Brazil has demonstrates more of external peace promotion trends meanwhile much is still needed within its internal governance. It follows that in recent years, even though Brazil has been implementing an increasingly assertive foreign policy, playing an active role in multilateral fora and positioning itself as a representative of emerging countries and as a staunch defender of poorer countries, particularly in Africa, and also has established a well developed political and institutional system, it however still has several limitations that are likely to have a negative effect on its internal governance, human rights and citizen's security. The country strategy paper highlights the following significant limitations:[27]

- The hurdles in the exercise of legislative and executive powers due to an inconsistent parliamentary mechanism that could appropriately coordinate the parliamentary majorities into the current political system. This defect maybe detrimental to the dynamic and quick execution of legislative responsibilities in service for the people and control over the abusive consequential actions of the executive and judiciary and also obviously slow certain governance dispositions

---

[27] See Brazil (2007-2013: 7).

thereby indirectly perpetrating the denial of timely justice to the people;

- The relative fragility within the Federal, the State and the Municipal levels of government thus making it difficult for the effective placements and implementation of nationwide policies and reforms. The effect of this maybe at one point at the level of promoting national integration and encouraging balanced development of the country's regional divisions, and at another point, promote delays, ethnic favouritism and governance neglects which are influential conflict promoter elements;

---

[28] In 2004 Transparency International ranked Brazil 59th out of 146 countries in its corruption perception index.

- The frequency in corruption[28] cases and misappropriation of public funds which are also conflict catalyst factors;

- The complex nature of the country's legal and regulatory mechanism that still need some functional improvement dynamics apt enough to improve the judiciary system, increase the efficiency of the public administration and enable citizens and economic operators fully to exercise their rights;

- The excessive use of force by law enforcement officials, limited access to justice for the poorest and most vulnerable sectors of society, and abuse against indigenous people are other major causes of concern which thus highlights the need to improve effective implementation of the existing legislation in the field of human rights [29]; and

- The violence crises in the country, which is particularly serious in big cities and frequently associated with (illegal) drug trafficking and social exclusion, generating a strong feeling of insecurity amongst citizens.

The Institutionalized Peaceful Development Tract of the Other Emerging Nations

Besides the examined case of China above, the other emerging nations also have adopted or institutionalized a number of proceedings that are contributive to the growth of in-country, continental and world peace as well.

---

[29] See the United Nations Human Rights' Committee considerations on the second periodic report of Brazil (CCPR/C/BRA/CO/2).

In the case of Brazil, as an emerging nation that has been highly active in maintaining privileged bilateral relations with neighbouring countries and has signed several trade agreements with others meanwhile establishing closer links not only with other regional powers and emerging nations such as India, China, Russia or South Africa but also with Arab or African countries[30], Brazil's internal peace growth institutionalization process has still not yet been as efficiently constituted like that of China. However, it's relatively stabilized and generalized national peace could be said as held in the religion of 'economic self-satisfaction believe systems' which I described above.

In the case of South Africa, for a country that has gone through such a horrible history of

---

[30] See Brazil (2007-2013: 8).

the apartheid era and presently instituted a peace development tract that is worthy of the emerging nation's circle, is a real example for the world to learn from. The institutionalization of a peace development tract in South Africa, is a process that begun since the end of the apartheid system between Nelson Mandela and F.W de Kleck.

The very primary institutional mechanisms for achieving and maintaining peace in South Africa after de Klerk's reign in 1994 to the triumph of Mandela was the creation of a truth and reconciliation commission[31] chaired by Archbishop Desmond Tutu, a widely respected Nobel Prize winner. The TRC provided a forum where any who had been a victim could tell their stories and be heard, and where those who perpetrated

---

[31] Promotion of National Unity and Reconciliation Act, Number 34 of 1995.

political violence could be granted amnesty from prosecution in exchange for full, honest disclosure. In a more concise manner, the postamble to the Interim Constitution of 1993, which made the granting of amnesty mandatory on the first democratic government of South Africa, stipulated that:

- The pursuit of national unity, the well-being of all South African citizens and peace require reconciliation between the people of South Africa and the reconstruction of society;

- The adoption of this Constitution lays the secure foundation for the people of South Africa to transcend the divisions and strife of the past, which generated gross violations of human rights, the transgression of humanitarian principles in violent conflicts and a legacy of hatred, fear, guilt and revenge; and

• These can now be addressed on the basis that there is a need for understanding but not for vengeance, a need for reparation but not for retaliation, a need for ubuntu but not for victimization.

In contrast to the situation of formerly discussed Brazil, the foundational basis for peace in an Emerging nation such as South Africa is a highly classical example of a moralized ethical peace institutionalized process wherein there is true prove that justice is tempered with mercy based on the principles of equity. In the case of Brazil, I tried to highlight the fact that because of the current periodic conflicts that are due to excessive use of force by the law enforcement officials and the illegal trafficking of drugs with the cities—yet the country still maintained an overall level of peace and stability, may have been due to the proposed religion view of the 'economic self-satisfaction believe systems'. However, for South Africa, though the country continues to struggle with severe problems of poverty, HIV/AIDS, crime and violence, it is still generally regarded as the most economically developed and socially advanced nation on the African continent. The case of its peace and stability is different to that of Brazil by the fact that it has demonstrated a true institutional mechanism for interpersonal and intercommunity solidarity and unity focus that has not been based on its economic progress for achieving the country's peace but on respect and tolerance of each and everyone's differences.

As one of the emerging nations who's internal country's peace building and stabilization process is particularly exceptional and exemplar for both the developing and the developed nations, its institutionalized peace development tract has not only been focused or limited within its territorial boundaries but has to a great extend engaged at diversified levels towards development assistance of other African countries. The country's engagement for its continent is based on three pillars:[32]

1) Strengthening Africa's institutions, regionally and continentally—more precisely entails Strengthening Africa's regional (South African Customs Union, SACU and Southern African Development Community, SADC) and continental (African Union, AU) institutions by enhancing South Africa's proactive participation in these bodies

---

[32] See Wolfe Braude, Pearl Thandrayan, Elizabeth Sidiropoulos (2008: 5).

aimed at promoting integration and development;

2) Supporting implementation of Africa's socioeconomic development program, the New Partnership for Africa's Development (NEPAD)—in precise terms entails supporting the implementation of Africa's socio-economic development programme, the New Partnership for Africa's Development (NEPAD) and of the SADC's Regional Indicative Strategic Development Plan (RISDP), the regional expression of Nepad; and

3) Improving bilateral political and socioeconomic relations through dialogue and cooperation—strengthening bilateral relations through effective structures for dialogue and cooperation. This includes support for peace, security, stability and

post-conflict reconstruction initiatives and South Africa's participation in the implementation of Africa's peace and security agenda and the management of peace missions.

Within South Africa's peace and security agenda, we can sight two major focuses that seem to shape the country's interventionist legitimacy. The first is observed by Flemes when he writes that 'the outstanding feature of foreign policy in the post-apartheid era indeed has been South Africa's identification and engagement with the rest of Africa'[33], the second is the evolving nature of conflict and security challenges, primarily but not exclusively on the African continent as 'policized' in the government's 1999 White Paper on South African Participation in International Peace

---

[33] See Flemes, D. (2007: 19).

Missions notes— 'a radically altered post Cold - War security environment has seen the transformation (or mutation) of classical peacekeeping operations into complex, multidimensional conflict management activities'.[34] Therefore, as a model nation for conflict resolution instances within the continent and beyond, South Africa emphasizes the importance of building and strengthening governance. Through preventive diplomacy, peacebuilding and peacemaking, it mostly stresses on the need for 'peace missions' over 'peacekeeping', the former being more inclusive, and embracing the principle that conflict resolution is first and foremost a political, rather than a military, project and that 'in all

---

[34] See White Paper on South African Participation in International Peace Missions, South African Department of Foreign Affairs, 1999. Avalaible online at
http://www.info.gov.za/view/DownloadFileAction?id=70438 pg. 4

cases, peace missions should aim at the empowerment of peoples and be based on local traditions and experiences, rather than the imposition of foreign modes of conflict management and governance'[35]. 'Although South Africa acknowledges its global responsibilities, the prioritization afforded Africa in South African foreign policy makes Africa the prime focus of future engagements', —perhaps as the only outstanding emerging nation in the conflict vulnerable sub-Saharan Africa— 'South Africa has an obvious interest in preserving regional peace and stability in order to promote trade and development and to avoid the spillover effects of conflicts in the neighbourhood'[36]

---

[35] Ibid. 19

[36] Ibid. 20

To the effect of the country's determination in dissolving conflicts in Africa and as the world's most referred to exemplary nation in which true dialogue had successfully braced the path to success in achieving an almost impossible peaceful situation in the country and also as an emergent nation whose goal is partly attached to bringing peace to other African under developed or developing nation States, some of South African's peace promoting initiative within the continent could be counted amongst the following:[37]

- Negotiating a major groundbreaking peace agreement in the Great Lakes Region signed between the governments of DRC and Rwanda which will facilitate the withdrawal of Rwandan troop in the DRC, the disarming and repatriation of

---

[37] See Aziz Pahad (2002:).

the Intarhamwe and ex-FAR. It is commented that the signing of this agreement has laid a solid foundation for security in the Great Lakes region thus enforcing South Africa's determination to promote peace, security and stability in this region;

- Hosting and promoting the adoption of the February-April 2002 Inter-Congolese Dialogue upon 40 resolutions in which was held major peace development ideologies such as the integration of opposing armed forces, the economic reconstruction of the country, national reconciliation and a humanitarian assistance programme;

- Assisting in the national reconciliation, reconstruction and unity in Angola through the approval of humanitarian assistance and relief for coping up with the humanitarian disaster in the country especially after the normalization of relations between both countries that followed the signing of the Luéna Cease-fire Accord in April 2002 by the People's Movement for the Liberation of Angola – Labour Party (MPLA) and National Union for the Total Independence of Angola (UNITA).

From the three examined examples of emerging nations' contributive ends in the institutionalization of peace and stability within other less developed or developing countries, it is possible to imply that, one of the most prioritized stamina of these countries include their determination towards building positive growth perspectives and solidifying partnership economies with developing nations which in one way or the other will foster peaceful and sustained bilateral trade for the well-being and development of both parties.

The Future of Peace within the Global Politics of Emerging Nations

After the careful examination of one of the most prominent bilateral goals of emerging nations, the probable conclusion may tie with the fact that in the advent of a full global empowerment of these emerging nations in one direction, the other developing countries may actually see the dawn of a more peaceful world especially within the poorest countries. Eventually, as time evolves, a new vision has been made manifest through the visionary institution of a new world order development bank called the BRICS Bank that will obviously challenge the World Bank. Smith writes that:

> Five giants of the developing world
> have in principle agreed to create a
> development bank to provide initial

funding for infrastructure projects worth $4.5tn (£3tn), in a potentially historic challenge to western-dominated financial institutions.[38]

The BRICS is a conglomerate of five emerging countries—Brazil, Russia, India, China, and South Africa created in the interest to promote mutual economic development amongst member nations. The original vision for the then BRIC bloc was borne out of the global financial crisis. Brazil, India, China and Russia seeking to distance themselves from the economic woes of the West, and to become less dependent on the volatility of the US dollar and the euro. With the invitation of South Africa two years ago - in part as a gateway to the wider continent, together BRICS nations now make up more

---

[38] See Smith, David (2013).

than 40 percent of the world's population - almost three billion people. The bloc generates one-fifth of the world's gross domestic product, and the World Bank says it is driving half of the global economic growth.[39] Though some of the main problems of BRICS group remain in the divergence of interests and perceptions on various issues such as to which member state to host the capital and also concerns on the contribution sums of the individual member states, one prominent concern in this study is that such a giant initiative will only lead into the speedy emergent development of the member states and obviously a more vigorous promotion of their development policy values.

As an effective platform of emerging economies through which natural resources,

---

[39] Aljazeera (2013).

intellectual power, cheap labors, great demography, spreading of modern technologies, military industrial complex which are all essential parts of development in modern era and are also very much present in the uniting nations, and further still hosting over 40% of global population, near about 30% of global economy and with 4% real GDP growth(whereas G7 countries have just 0.7% GDP growth), and by large land-mass, the BRICS has every possibility to have a robust foot print in coming days multi-polar world order.[40] It also goes that these emerging economies are not 'free riders, and will continue to play a more active role in international affairs, said by a senior Foreign Ministry official told a global security forum.[41]

---

[40] See http://therussianangle.wordpress.com/tag/brics-for-emerging-nations/ retrieved on the 30th of May 2013.

[41] See

With most of the member states (especially South Africa and China) active internal policies to support peace and conflict resolution the world over and especially in sub-Saharan Africa, it is no major worry that the maintenance and enforcement of such their international policy issues will, to a great extend, change the course and story line of conflicts in Africa.

They have also been major debates upon issues of the BRIC in analyzing how the rapid growth of a large number of developing countries represented by China, India, Brazil, South Africa and Indonesia in recent years will shape the future of the world order. If emerging economies have been calling for a reform in the international economic and financial order to increase the representation

http://www.nytimes.com/2013/03/28/world/middleeast/syrias-developments.html?_r=0

of developing countries, then there is hope for more developing economies and hope for true democratic values within most of the authoritarian rules within the heart of Africa. In support to the ideal of developing nations' responsibilities against that of developed nations, Zhang Yuyan, director of the Institute of World Economy and Politics at the Chinese Academy of Social Sciences said that 'It's necessary to differentiate responsibilities between developed countries and developing countries, especially in issues caused by historical reasons, like the emission of carbon dioxide,' meanwhile still seeing the need for mutual trust to be built up between developed and developing countries.[42] The emphasis on the separation of responsibilities posed by Zhang could as well be calculated on

---

[42] See ibid.

the division of the global development responsibility in order to foster an egalitarian focus on the development priorities of the lower developing countries. The BRICS bank within this scope, needs more policy strategy reforms with regards their investment priorities such that their priority focus will be to promote peace and economic growth within other developing nations in line to assist in pulling along these lower degree developing nations up to the global competitive standards in political governance, human rights and moral justice which are the key principles for maintaining peace.

Given that the initial goal of this unity focus of the emerging nations - BRICS is to create an economic union with due respect to each other's sovereignty, we can however estimate that in future, they will have the opportunity to co-operate with each other on various regional assistance and security issues considering their growing in-country bilateral assistance development policies and military clout. One pertinent thing that stands forward is the fact that they need to resolve their foremost differences or to ignore such differences for greater interests and wellbeing of the unity. These could be carried out through media initiatives with respective media houses in member-states actively taking part in promoting the positive analytic views on union ideas, inter-cultural BRICS centres across the member countries for strengthening and reigniting their cultural ties; cross-member State scholar exchange programmes, scholarships, and facilitated immigration processes.

The BRICS Member States Specifics in Peace Initiatives

The emerging nations who now form the BRICS are all acknowledge as having firm standing on the promotion of regional and global peace initiatives. Even though their individual nations aspirations may stray on varying grounds, one thing for sure is the fact that their individual polices upon peacemaking are huge and may only grow wider with the coming of the BRICS bank. Considering Russia and South Africa's peace policy positions as the exemplary cases may give us a gestalt of the eventual outcome preview in peace operations should the BRICS rise to a full world order positioning.

The Case of Russia. Predominantly and from some historical ties perspectives since the collapse of the Soviet Union, Russia's policy has often been to cement peace within the former soviet territories. Thus, its peace plan is highly focused on its desire to be the regional peacemaker within the zone. This role was enforced by the rise to power of President Vladimir Putin, who led Russia towards a proactive security role, with the quest to develop the Collective Security Treaty Organization (CSTO) into the preeminent regional security organization in Eurasia, recognized by the UN and with a mandate to undertake peacekeeping, including interventions within its member states. Worth remaking is the fact that Russia has little direct interest in international peace operations, except in so far as to prevent them from becoming tools for Western strategic interests—however it still has indicated its willingness to increase financial support for UN peace operations.[43]

The Case of South Africa. Already extensively discussed in a previous section of this study, South Africa's approach to peace operations has been closely aligned with its ambitions to assert itself as Africa's regional leader and gain access to leading international forums (e.g. the G20).[44] The country's key political aim has been the promotion of an African renaissance through the New Economic Partnership for Africa's Development (NEPAD).[45] By several of the Country's policy goals, there may be a considerate believe that there is a link between African stability and South African prosperity. This is through the nation's involvements in mediation initiatives

---

[43] See Nikitin, A. (2011).

[44] See South African Government, *Building a Better World: the Diplomacy of Ubunto*, 13 May 2011, <http://www.info.gov.za/view/DownloadFileAction?id=14974 9>, p. 4.

[45] See Kornegay, F.(2011).

and providing significant military contributions to UN and AU-led peace operations. In a similitude to the Russian values against Western manipulations through peace operations, South Africa's own point of view streams from fact that it has sought to shield African countries from what it sees as overly aggressive Western (colonial) policies and has avoided criticizing other African leaders. Meanwhile it has also accepted the principle of UN peacekeeping, its support has been tied to national interests.[46]

---

[46] See Sharon Wiharta, Neil Melvin and Xenia Avezov (2012).

Conclusion

The high development rate and global support for peace operations in both regional and global spectrums demonstrated by the emerging nations are true legendary moves when we consider their historical backgrounds of violence and political instability, but astonishingly, these emerging nations are well-known for their high levels of corruption within their internal economic management processes as accessed by transparency international. Also, in several occasions and in many philosophical viewpoints, corruption has been defined as a total destroyer of development and disrespect for human rights, thus a high conflict making catalyst. The worry here now is, in the advent of these emergent nations' to a world order,

either through the formation of the BRICS
bank or through their highly influential
regional peace initiatives and bilateral
economic cooperation with other less
developed and more vulnerable countries,
*wouldn't these vulnerable countries'
situations become worse as in the induced
corruption habits they may copy from their
benefactor nations?*

However, as much as the emerging
nations generally strategize in supporting
the peaceful coexistence and national
solidarity within regional dimensions, they
also need to fight against the spread of
some of their in-countries' depraved
amorality habits such as that of corruption
towards the more vulnerable developing
nations who do not yet have the aptitude to
withstand its impacts. Nonobservance the

critical position, in general, the growing
policy movements of emerging nations
towards peaceful operations are highly
consolidated global phenomena. Nicholas
Stern et al write that:

> A development bank anchored in
> emerging markets and
> developing countries can help to
> address this gap and become a
> powerful catalyst for change,
> both in the developing world and
> – through collaboration and
> example – in existing
> institutions....the World Bank
> and the regional development
> banks now recognize such
> imperatives, and the New
> Development Bank should not
> relieve the developed countries

of their responsibilities. But, with the shortfall of assistance from developed to developing countries, the new bank can provide essential help to developing countries and emerging markets as they undertake smarter and more sustainable infrastructure investment for growth and poverty reduction. Given the need to act quickly – and given the slowness with which the developed world has been responding – this new institution is all the more welcome. [47]

---

[47] See Nicholas Stern, Amar Bhattacharya, Mattia Romani, Joseph E. Stiglitz (2013).

References

Aljazeera (2013). BRICS: Challenging the global economic order. Available online at: http://www.aljazeera.com/programmes/insidestory/2013/03/201332855326683703.html retrieved on the 30th of May 2013

Aziz Pahad (2002). Towards Peace and Stability In The Continent Of Africa. Progress Report on issues Raised during the President Thabo Mbeki's State of the Nation Address and a Follow-Up on the Decisions of the Mid-Year Cabinet Lekgotla14 August 2002-08-19. Available pdf online at: http://www.sarpn.org/NEPAD/pahad/Pahad.pdf retrieved on the 30th of May 2013.

Banerjee, A. and E. Duflo (2007). "What is Middle Class about the Middle Classes

Around the World?" MIT Department of
Economics Working Paper 07-29,
Cambridge, MA.

Barro, R. (1996). 'Determinants of
Economic Growth: A Cross-Country
Empirical Study', NBER Working Paper
5698, National Bureau of Economic
Research Inc., Cambridge, MA.

Brazil (2007-2013). Country Strategy
Paper 2007-2013. European Commission
14.05.2007 (E/2007/889)

Doyle, Michael W. (1983). "Kant, Liberal
Legacies, and Foreign Affairs". *Philosophy
and Public Affairs* **12** (Vol. 12, No. 3.
(Summer, 1983)): 205–235.
JSTOR 2265298.

Flemes, D. (2007). "Conceptualising
Regional Power in International Relations:
Lessons from the South African Case,"

GIGA Working Papers No. 53, German
Institute of Global and Area Studies, June
2007, p. 7.

IMF (2009). 'Q. How does the WEO
categorize advanced versus emerging and
developing economies?'. International
Monetary Fund. Available online at:
http://www.imf.org/external/pubs/ft/weo/fa
q.htm#q4b Retrieved July 20, 2009.

IMF (2012). World Economic Outlook
Database, April 2012. Available online at:
http://www.imf.org/external/pubs/ft/weo/20
12/01/weodata/weorept.aspx?pr.x=82&pr.y
=8&sy=2011&ey=2011&scsm=1&ssd=1&s
ort=country&ds=.&br=1&c=193%2C158%
2C122%2C542%2C124%2C137%2C156%2
C181%2C423%2C138%2C935%2C196%2C
128%2C142%2C939%2C182%2C172%2C5
76%2C132%2C936%2C134%2C961%2C17

4%2C184%2C532%2C144%2C176%2C146
%2C178%2C528%2C436%2C112%2C136%
2C111&s=NGDPD%2CPPPGDP&grp=0&
a= Accessed on the 28th of May 2013.

Kornegay, F.(2011). 'Emerging power
engagement in development and security:
South Africa's "Peace and Security"
perspective on conflict-affected states', eds
J. Sherman, M. M. Gleason, W. P. S. Sidhu
and B. Jones, *Engagement on Development
and Security: New Actors, New Debates*
(Center on International Cooperation:
New York, 2011), p. 41.

Mauro F. Guillén (2003).
'Multinationals, Ideology, and Organized
Labor'. *The Limits of Convergence*.
Princeton University Press. ISBN 0-691-
11633-4.

Mankiw, N. Gregory (4th Edition
2007). *Principles of Economics.* ISBN 0-
324-22472-9.

Nicholas Stern, Amar Bhattacharya,
Mattia Romani, Joseph E. Stiglitz
*(2013). A New World's New Development
Bank.* Available online at:
http://www.project-
syndicate.org/commentary/the-benefits-of-
the-brics-development-bank . *Retrieved on
the 31st of May 2013*

Nikitin, A. (2011). 'Russia's participation
in international peacekeeping', *Security
Index: A Russian Journal on International
Security*, vol. 17, no. 3, 2011, pp. 43–44

Parker, John (2009-02-12). "Special
report: Burgeoning bourgeoisie". *The
Economist* (2009-02-13).
http://www.economist.com/specialreports/d

isplayStory.cfm?story_id=13063298&sourc
e=hptextfeature . Accessed on the 29th of
May 2013.

Paweł Bożyk (2006). 'Newly
Industrialized Countries'. *Globalization
and the Transformation of Foreign
Economic Policy*. Ashgate Publishing, Ltd.
ISBN 0-7546-4638-6.

People's Daily (2005-10-22). 'Full Text:
China's Peaceful Development Road'.
Available online at:
http://english.peopledaily.com.cn/200512/2
2/eng20051222_230059.html. Retrieved on
the 29th of May 2013

Qu Xing (2013). An Emerging China in
Pursuit of Peace and Prosperity. China
Institute for International Studies.
Available online at:
http://www.ciis.org.cn/english/2013-

05/02/content_5919530.htm retrieved on
the 29th of May 2013

**Sharon Wiharta, Neil Melvin and
Xenia Avezov (2012).** *South Africa: A
'Renaissance' Peacekeeper?* Mapping The
Emerging Landscape. The New Geopolitics
Of Peace Operations. Stockholm
International Peace Research Institute.
September 2012 pg. 9

Smith, David (2013). 'Brics eye
infrastructure funding through new
development bank'. The Guardian.
Available online at :
http://www.guardian.co.uk/global-
development/2013/mar/28/brics-countries-
infrastructure-spending-development-
bank Retrieved 30th of May 2013.

**Sullivan, Arthur; Steven M. Sheffrin
(2003).** *Economics: Principles in Action.*

Upper Saddle River, New Jersey 07458:
Pearson Prentice Hall. p. 471. ISBN 0-13-
063085-3.

The Global Middle Class (2009). Views
on Democracy, Religion, Values, and Life
Satisfaction in Emerging Nation. The Pew
Global Attitudes Project . February 12
2009 release. Webstie. www.pewglobal.org

Waugh, David (3rd edition 2000).
'Manufacturing industries (chapter 19),
World development (chapter 22)'.
Geography, An Integrated Approach.
Nelson Thornes Ltd. pp. 563, 576–579,
633, and 640. ISBN 0-17-444706-X.

**Wolfe Braude, Pearl Thandrayan,
Elizabeth Sidiropoulos (2008).**
Emerging Donors in International
Development Assistance: The South Africa

Case. South African Institute of
International Affairs.